The
Fish
Classes

Family Trees

The Fish Classes

REBECCA STEFOFF

 **Marshall Cavendish**
Benchmark
New York

With thanks to Paul L. Sieswerda, Aquarium Curator, New York Aquarium, for his expert review of the manuscript.

Marshall Cavendish Benchmark
99 White Plains Road
Tarrytown, New York 10591-9001
www.marshallcavendish.us
Text copyright © 2008 by Rebecca Stefoff
Illustrations copyright © 2008 by Marshall Cavendish Corporation
Illustrations by Robert Romagnoli

Editor: Karen Ang
Publisher: Michelle Bisson
Art Director: Anahid Hamparian
Series Designer: Patrice Sheridan

Library of Congress Cataloging-in-Publication Data

Stefoff, Rebecca, date
The fish classes / by Rebecca Stefoff.
p. cm. — (Family trees)
Summary: "Explores the habitats, life cycles, and other characteristics of animals in the Fish classes"—
Provided by publisher.
Includes bibliographical references and index.
ISBN 978-0-7614-2695-0
1. Fishes–Juvenile literature. I. Title. II. Series.

QL617.2.S694 2008
597—dc22

2007003483

Front cover: Two pink anemonefish live among the tentacles of a sea anemone.
Title page: A seahorse; Page 7: A French grunt; Page 19: A treefish; Page 33: A butterflyfish;
Back cover: A pufferfish.

Photo research by Candlepants, Incorporated
Cover Photo: Becca Saunders/AUSCAPE / Minden Pictures
The photographs in this book are used by permission and through the courtesy of: *Minden Pictures:* Norbert Wu, 3, 21, 26, 45, 51, 56, 60, 71, 72, 76; Chris Newbert, 6, 52, 67, 73, 74; Constantios Petrinos/npl, 18; Fred Bavendam, 30, 61, 66; Flip Nicklin, 48, 49, 57, 63; Stephen Dalton, 64; Frans Lanting, 68; Hiroya Minakuchi, 85. *Marshall Cavendish:* 7, 19, 33. *The Bridgeman Art Library:* © Royal Asiatic Society, London, UK, 10. *Corbis:* David Gray/Reuters, 12; Jonathon Blair, 39; Reuters, 42; China Newsphoto/Reuters, 78; Jeffrey L. Rotman, 81; Natalie Fobes, 82. *Photo Researchers Inc.:* Shelia Terry, 9; Tom McHugh, 23, 47, 45, 53, 84; David Hall, 24; Gary Meszaros, 25; Dirk Wiersma, 32; Michael Neumann, 34; James L. Amos, 36; Christian Darkin, 38; Peter Scoones, 43. *Animals Animals:* Chris McLaughlin, 44, back cover; James Watt, 54; Breck P. Kent, 59. *Visuals Unlimited:* David Wrobel, 46, 70; Patrice Ceisel, 55. *AP Images:* Ed Wray, 80 (right); Alex Dorgan-Ross, 80 (left).

Printed in Malaysia
1 3 5 6 4 2

CONTENTS

The white-ringed spots on the tail of this ocellated lionfish look like eyes. By confusing or frightening possible predators, the spots help protect the lionfish. They are an example of protective coloration.

Classifying Life

If you row out onto a lake for a typical day of fishing, you might see four or five different kinds of fish. If you go snorkeling or scuba diving in a rich underwater habitat, such as a kelp forest or tropical reef, you could spot dozens of species. And if you visit a large, well-stocked aquarium, you could see hundreds of species, from huge sharks that cast sinister shadows as they glide through the water to tiny neon-colored fish that spend their lives tucked into crevices in corals.

But that's just a small fraction of the world of fish. The water that covers more than two-thirds of Earth's surface is home to a vast variety of fish (and many other kinds of creatures as well). More than 28,000 species of fish are known, and more are identified all the time. The number of fish species is greater than that of amphibian, reptile, bird, and mammal species added together. Fish were around long before those four groups existed—in fact, all of them evolved *from* fish. Ichthyologists, as scientists who study fish are called, sometimes point out that all land-dwelling animals, including human beings, are just a small side branch in the ongoing story of fish evolution. To understand the place of fish in the animal kingdom, it helps to know something about how scientists classify living things.

THE INVENTION OF TAXONOMY

Science provides tools for making sense of the natural world. One of the most powerful tools is classification, which means organizing things in a pattern according to their differences and similarities. Since ancient times, scientists who study plants and animals have been developing taxonomy, a classification system for living things. Taxonomy groups together plants or animals that share certain features, and sets them apart from other plants and animals with different features.

Taxonomy is hierarchical, which means that it is arranged in levels of categories. The highest levels include many kinds of organisms. These large categories are divided into smaller ones, which in turn are divided into still smaller ones. The smallest category of all is the species, a single kind of organism. The idea behind taxonomy is simple, but the world of living things is complex and full of surprises. Taxonomy is not a fixed pattern. It keeps changing to reflect new knowledge or ideas. Over time, scientists have developed rules for adjusting that pattern even when they disagree on its details.

One of the first taxonomists was the ancient Greek philosopher Aristotle (384-322 BCE), who investigated many branches of science, including biology. Aristotle arranged living things on a sort of ladder, or scale. At the bottom were those he considered lowest, or least developed, such as worms. Above them were things he considered higher, or more developed, such as fish, then birds, then mammals. Aristotle was an early ichthyologist. He described 117 kinds of Mediterranean Sea fish so accurately that scientists today can identify the species.

For centuries after Aristotle, taxonomy made little progress. People who studied nature tended to group organisms together by obvious features, such as separating trees from grasses or birds from fish. However, they did not try to develop a system for classifying all life. Then, between 1682 and 1705, an English naturalist named John Ray published a plan of the living world that was designed to have a place for every species of plant and animal. Part of Ray's study of all living things was his 1686 book

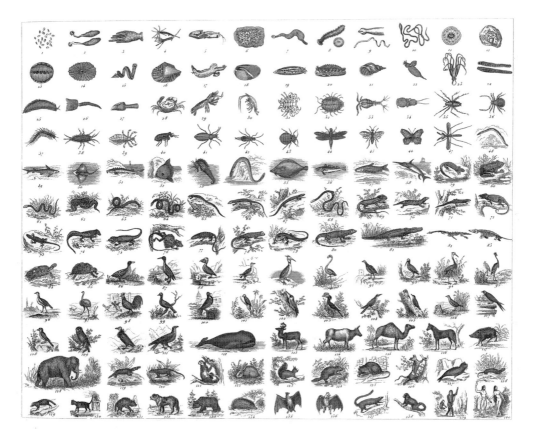

Taxonomists used to rank living things from primitive to advanced, as shown on this 1860 chart. Microscopic organisms (top left) were thought to be the simplest forms of life, while human beings (bottom right) were considered the most "advanced."

Historia Piscium (The History of Fishes), written with his fellow naturalist Francis Willughby. It described 420 species and arranged them into categories. Ray's system of organizing living things was hierarchical, with several levels of larger and smaller categories. It was the foundation of modern taxonomy. Swedish naturalist Carolus Linnaeus (1707-1778) built on that foundation to create the taxonomic system used today.

Linnaeus was chiefly interested in plants, but his system of classification included all living things. The highest level of classification was the kingdom. To Linnaeus, everything belonged to either the plant or the animal kingdom. Each of these kingdoms was divided into a number of smaller categories called classes. Each class was divided into orders. Each order was divided into genera. Each genus (the singular form of genera) contained one or more species.

One of Linnaeus's colleagues and friends, Peter Artedi (1705–1735), has been called the "father of ichthyology." Artedi studied fish species and developed a classification system for them. He drowned at the age of thirty before publishing any of his work, but Linnaeus acquired Artedi's notes and published them. Linnaeus used Artedi's system of fish classification as part of his own larger classification of living things.

Nonscientists have made many important contributions to natural history. These drawings of Chinese fish species were made by a nineteenth-century artist.

Linnaeus also developed another of John Ray's ideas, a method for naming species. Before Linnaeus published his important work *System of Nature* in 1735, scientists had no recognized system for referring to plants and animals. Organisms were generally known by their common names, but many of them had different names in different countries. As a result, naturalists often called the same plant or animal by different names. Sometimes they used the same name to refer to different organisms.

Linnaeus wanted to end such confusion and allow scholars everywhere to communicate clearly when writing about plants and animals. He established the practice of giving each plant or animal a two-part scientific name consisting of its genus and species, both in Latin, which was the scientific language of Linnaeus's day. The Antarctic spiny plunderfish, for example, has the scientific name *Harpagifer bispinis* (or *H. bispinis* after the first time the full name is used). This fish belongs to the genus *Harpagifer,* which includes other kinds of Antarctic plunderfishes. The second part of the name, *bispinis,* refers only to the spiny plunderfish.

Linnaeus named hundreds of species. Other scientists quickly adopted his highly flexible system to name thousands more. The Linnaean system appeared at a time when European naturalists were exploring the rest of the world, finding thousands of new plants and animals. This flood of discoveries was overwhelming at times, but Linnaean taxonomy helped scientists identify and organize their finds for systematic study.

TAXONOMY TODAY

Biologists still use the system of scientific naming that Linnaeus developed (anyone who discovers a new species can choose its scientific name, which is almost always in Latin, although a few names are Greek). Other aspects of taxonomy, though, have changed since Linnaeus's time.

As biologists learned more about living things, they added new levels to taxonomy to reflect their growing understanding of the similarities and

Douglas Hoese, retired chief scientist of the Australian Museum, examines a newly discovered goby found in ocean caves near Australia and Japan. The fish's species name will honor Emperor Akihito of Japan, an enthusiastic student of biology.

differences among organisms. Eventually, an organism's full classification could include the following taxonomic levels: kingdom, subkingdom, phylum (for animals) or division (sometimes used for plants and fungi), subphylum or subdivision, superclass, class, subclass, infraclass, order, superfamily, family, genus, species, and subspecies or variety.

Another change concerned the kinds of information that scientists use to classify organisms. The earliest naturalists used obvious physical features, such as the differences between reptiles and mammals, to divide organisms into general groups. By the time of Ray and Linnaeus, naturalists could study specimens in more detail. Aided by new tools such as the microscope, they explored the inner structures of plants and animals. For a long time after Linnaeus, classification was based mainly on details of anatomy, or physical structure, although scientists also looked at how an organism reproduced and how and where it lived.

Today, biologists can peer more deeply into an organism's inner workings than Aristotle or Linnaeus ever dreamed possible. They can look inside its individual cells and study the arrangement of DNA that makes up its genetic blueprint. Genetic information is key to modern classification because DNA is more than an organism's blueprint—it also contains clues to how closely that organism is related to other species, and how long ago those species separated during the process of evolution.

In recent years, many biologists have pointed out that the Linnaean system is a patchwork of old and new ideas. It doesn't clearly reflect the latest knowledge about evolutionary connections among organisms both living and extinct. Some scientists have adopted a new approach to taxonomy, one based entirely on evolutionary relationships. One of the most useful new approaches is called phylogenetics. This method groups together all organisms that are descended from the same ancestor using a technique called cladistics. Scientists arrange organisms in branching, tree-like diagrams called cladograms. These show the order in which groups of plants or animals split off from a line of shared ancestry.

Classifying the Great White Shark

One of the most famous—or notorious—fish is *Carcharodon carcharias*, the great white shark. The largest recorded specimen of this oceanic predator was a female 19.8 feet (7.1 m) long, weighing 5,060 pounds (2,300 kg). But one of the great white shark's extinct relatives reached lengths of up to 49.5 feet (15 m). Called *Carcharodon megalodon*, it was the largest predatory shark that ever swam. Here's how taxonomists classify these two mighty fish:

Kingdom	Animalia (animals)
Phylum	Chordata (with spinal cords)
Subphylum	Vertebrata (with segmented spines)
Superclass	Gnathostomata (vertebrates with jaws)
Class	Chondrichthyes (fish with skeletons made of cartilage: sharks and rays)
Order	Lamniformes (sharks with two dorsal fins, no spines, five gill slits, and large mouths)
Family	Lamnidae (mackerel sharks, porbeagles, white sharks)
Genus	*Carcharodon* (white sharks)
Species	*carcharias* (great white shark) or *megalodon* (now extinct)

Although none of the proposed new systems of classifying living things has yet been agreed upon by all scientists, the move toward a phylogenetic approach is under way. Most experts recognize the importance of cladistics while still using the two main features of Linnaean taxonomy: the hierarchy of categories and the two-part species name. Yet scientists may disagree about the proper term for a category, or hold conflicting views about the classification of a particular plant or animal. Experts often debate whether two organisms belong to the same species or to different species, or whether an organism represents a new species.

Even at the highest level of classification, not all scientists agree on a single, final taxonomy. A few of them still divide all life into two kingdoms, plants and animals. Others divide life into as many as thirteen kingdoms. Most scientists, though, use systems of classification that have five or six kingdoms: plants, animals, fungi, and two or three kingdoms of microscopic organisms such as bacteria, amoebas, and algae.

Plant and animal classifications change often as scientists apply new evolutionary or genetic insights to taxonomy. Fish, for example, used to be considered a single class of animals, called Pisces in Latin. Today, though, most experts recognize five classes of living fishes (and more classes of extinct ones). In recent decades, ichthyologists have revised fish taxonomy again and again. Traditional Linnaean classification—a series of nested levels, with each level completely contained in the level above it—doesn't work well for fish, because any category that is broad enough to include *all* fish must also include a lot of things that aren't fish, such as hummingbirds and hippopotamuses. "Fish" as a single, all-inclusive category has little scientific meaning. Instead, ichthyologists focus on the remarkably rich variety of classes, orders, and families of these ancient, adaptable swimmers.

Scientists classify living things in arrangements like this family tree of the animal

ANIMAL

PHYLA

CNIDARIANS

Coral

ARTHROPODS
(Animals with external skeletons and jointed limbs)

MOLLUSKS

Octopus

SUB PHYLA

CLASSES

CRUSTACEANS
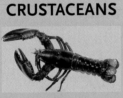
Lobster

ARACHNIDS

Spider

INSECTS

Butterfly

MYRIAPODS

Centipede

ORDERS

CARNIVORES

Bear

SEA MAMMALS
(2 ORDERS)

Dolphin

PRIMATES
Monkey

kingdom to highlight the connections and the differences among the many forms of life.

KINGDOM

ANNELIDS

Earthworm

CHORDATES

(Animals with a dorsal nerve chord)

ECHINODERMS

Starfish

VERTEBRATES

(Animals with a backbone)

FISH

Fish

BIRDS

Penguin

MAMMALS

AMPHIBIANS

Frog

REPTILES

Snake

HERBIVORES
(5 ORDERS)

Horse

RODENTS

Squirrel

INSECTIVORES

Hedgehog

MARSUPIALS

Kangaroo

SMALL MAMMALS
(SEVERAL ORDERS)

Rabbit

Perched on a branch of gorgonian coral in Indonesia, the pygmy seahorse blends into its surroundings. This tiny fish, which reaches lengths of about 1 inch (2 centimeters), is covered with bumps called tubercules that mimic the lumpy coral.

CHAPTER ONE

What Is a Fish?

Everyone knows what a fish is, right? Surprisingly, a "fish" is not as easy to define as you might think. A typical dictionary definition goes like this: "An aquatic vertebrate that breathes through gills and moves by using fins." Let's look at that definition piece by piece.

"Aquatic" means that the animal lives in water. (Those that live in saltwater may be called "marine.") Fish *are* aquatic—except for the mudskippers, which can live out of water for as long as thirty hours. They spend most of their time clambering around on the shore, pulling themselves along with their fins.

A "vertebrate" is an animal that has a backbone made of up individual segments called vertebrae. Nearly all species of fish do have segmented backbones, the part of the skeleton that covers and supports the sensitive nerves of the spinal cord. In some groups of fish, though, the backbone is made of a tough, rubbery material called cartilage rather than true bone. And hagfishes and lampreys have no backbone at all, just a notochord, a protective rod of flexible cells around the nerves.

All fish need oxygen, and all of them have gills, structures that allow oxygen from the water to enter their bloodstreams. But some fish can also breathe air, either through special blood vessels in their bodies or through lungs. To complicate things even more, creatures that aren't fish—certain kinds of salamanders and other amphibians—are also aquatic vertebrates that take oxygen through gills.

What about fins? All living fish species have fins, although some have more fins than others, and the fins of some species are small and hard to see. But fins are a sure sign of a true fish. They are one of the features that make fish so well suited to life in the water.

LIVING IN A WATERY WORLD

More than 70 percent of Earth's surface is covered by salt water. Only about 1 percent is covered by fresh water. Yet 41 percent of all known fish species live in fresh water, while 58 percent are marine, or saltwater, species. The remaining 1 percent move back and forth between fresh and salt water during their life cycles, or they live in places like river mouths, where salt and fresh water mix to form brackish water.

Marine fish are not distributed evenly through all parts of the oceans. About 78 percent of marine species—which account for 44 percent of all the fish in the world—live along the edges of the land masses, in water less than 660 feet (200 meters) deep. The 13 percent of marine species that live in the open ocean, far from land, are concentrated in warmer waters. Fish are ectothermic, or cold-blooded. This means that they do not produce their own body heat. Instead, their body temperatures are influenced by their environments. Because more fish species have evolved to survive in warm environments than in cold ones, the polar regions have the lowest numbers of species. Tropical regions have the most species. The region with the greatest number of species is the Indo-Pacific region, which stretches from the Red Sea eastward to Polynesia.

Different species also inhabit different levels of the water column—the vertical dimension of the sea from surface to bottom. Fishes that live in

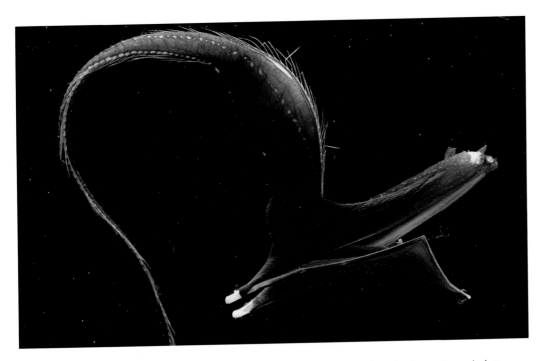

The deep-sea gulper, also called the pelican eel, has a long whiplike tail and a hinged mouth that opens wide to swallow large prey. It measures about 2 feet (61 cm) long and lives at depths greater than 6,500 feet (1,970 m).

the upper part of the water column, from the surface down to about 600 feet (183 m) or so, are called epipelagic. Those that live farther down are called bathypelagic. The greatest depth reached by sunlight is about 3,300 feet (1,000 m). More bathypelagic species live above that level, in water that receives at least dim light, than below it, in permanent darkness. But the bottom of the water column is home to a completely different community of species called the benthic fishes. They live on or near the ocean floor at depths of down to 22,000 feet (6,710 m).

Life in water has advantages and disadvantages. Water is about eight hundred times more dense than air. This means that water offers a lot more support to fish than air offers to birds. Fish don't have to work very hard to stay afloat at the depth that is right for them. However, swimming forward through water is more difficult than moving through air. Many fish have a streamlined, sleek body shape that cuts through the water with minimum resistance. Fish also have highly developed muscles along the sides of their bodies. These make their bodies ripple or wriggle slightly, pushing them through the water. The muscles also control fishes' fins, which are used for forward motion, braking, and changing direction.

Jacques Cousteau, a French underwater explorer who shared the wonders of the sea with a worldwide audience through books and television shows, published his first book about the sea in 1953. It was called *The Silent World*. People find the ocean a silent place because human ears don't work well in the water. To fish, though, the sea can be quite noisy. Sound travels farther and faster through water than through air, and many species of fish use it to communicate. They make a wide variety of sounds, and they "hear" through an inner ear that contains bony structures called otoliths.

FISHY FEATURES

Fins are the mark of a fish, but there is great variety in their size, shape, and position. Five kinds of fins exist, but not all fish have all five kinds. The dorsal fin runs along the top of the fish's back; some species have more than one of these. The anal fin is located on the underside of the body, near the fish's anus, or vent. The caudal fin is the tail. Most fishes also have pectoral and pelvic fins. The pectoral and pelvic fins occur in pairs, like the arms and legs (or wings and legs) of land-dwelling vertebrates. The pectoral fins are located behind the fish's head, one on each side. The pelvic fins, sometimes called ventral fins, are below or behind the pectoral fins.

In addition to an internal skeleton of bone or cartilage, many fishes have an external skeleton made of scales. On slow-moving fishes—species as varied as the large sturgeon and the tiny seahorse—scales may take the form of tough, bony, armor-like plates, sometimes only on part of the body.

The Russian sturgeon's scales are thick, armor-like plates. The growths on its upper lip are barbels, which are sense organs that help the fish find prey as it drifts along the bottom.

Faster-moving species usually have an all-over coating of thin, flexible, overlapping scales. Certain species, such as some eels and catfish, have no scales at all. Others, including many kinds of tuna, look as if they have no scales because their scales are buried in their skin.

Skin and scale coloring is highly variable. Many tropical reef fish are vividly patterned with brilliant colors in spots, splotches, and stripes. A plain blue-gray, however, is common in pelagic species. Darker coloration on the back than on the belly helps a fish blend into its background whether seen from above or below. Many fishes that live on the bottom have cryptic coloration—that is, colors and patterns that let them "disappear" into the rocks, sand, or weeds of their environment.

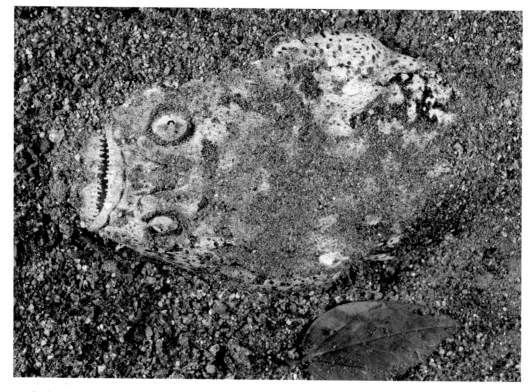

Only the eyes and the waiting mouth reveal that a flat fish called a marbled stargazer lurks beneath a layer of sand.

All fishes have a sense organ called the lateral-line system. It runs along each side of a fish's head and body, and it is made up of cells called neuromasts that react to slight changes in pressure caused by the movement of the water. The lateral-line system works like an extra sense of touch, letting fish "feel" movements and objects in the water. It alerts them when prey or predators are near, helps them steer through obstacles such as weeds or rocks, and lets fish that are swimming together in schools keep from bumping into one another or wandering off.

Fish have an array of other senses. Vision is highly varied. Many fish have keen eyesight, which they use for locating prey. Others, such as cave fish and hagfish, are practically blind, although they may be able to sense light. Fish also have senses of taste and smell. Taste buds are located on their bodies and fins as well as in their mouths. The water that enters a fish's nostrils passes over its organs of olfaction, or smell, and back out through the nostrils. All fish have an olfactory sense, but it is strongest in predatory fishes, such as the sharks.

Some of fishes' other senses are not yet well understood by scientists. Experts believe, for example, that many species can sense weak electrical currents, such as those produced by muscle movement in other animals. About five hundred species generate significant amounts of electricity. The torpedo ray, the electric catfish, and the electric eel are some of the fishes with special muscle groups that produce steady low-level electrical fields or sudden strong jolts of electricity. These fish also have electroreceptors, cells that are especially sensitive to other fishes' electrical signals.

On these redside dace, the sense organ called the lateral line is clearly visible. It is the pale streak just above the reddish patch.

Seen here from below, *Torpedo californica* is an electric ray that makes its home in the underwater kelp forests off North America's Pacific coast.

The low-level electrical fields help the fish communicate with others of the same species. They are also used in getting around. A fish uses electricity like radar, sending out electrical pulses and "reading" its surroundings from changes in the electrical field around it. Strong jolts, though, are used for attacking prey or for defense against attackers. An electric eel can produce as much as 650 volts of electricity, enough to kill a good-sized fish or animal. People have been killed by multiple electric eel shocks, although such deaths are rare.

The swim bladder is a special organ found in the majority of fish species. It is a pouch inside the upper part of the fish's body that is filled with gas—either air that the fish has gulped at the surface, or gases produced by the fish's own body. The main purpose of the swim bladder is to help the fish adjust its buoyancy, helping it float at a steady depth without using much energy. Because gas is lighter than water, the right amount of gas in a swim bladder offsets the weight of the fish, which can then float as if weightless.

Swim bladders do more than help fish control buoyancy. In some species they are connected to the inner ear. They act like an echo chamber, improving the fish's hearing. Other species use their swim bladders as lungs or as mechanisms to make sounds. The bladders are lined with blood vessels that can absorb oxygen from air gulped at the surface. Scientists think that swim bladders started out as lungs in early groups of fishes and later evolved into buoyancy-control organs in some species.

A FISH'S EXTERNAL FEATURES

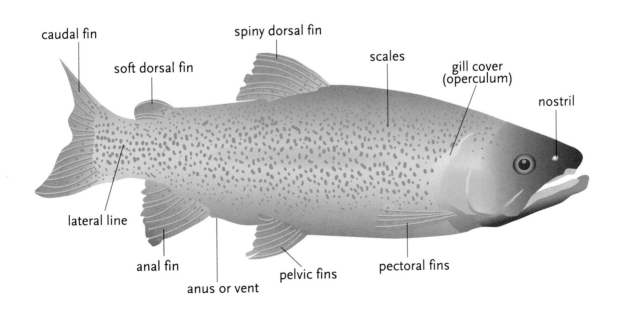

caudal fin

spiny dorsal fin

soft dorsal fin

scales

gill cover (operculum)

nostril

lateral line

anal fin

anus or vent

pelvic fins

pectoral fins

Form and Function

Fish come in an immense variety of shapes. Each class of fishes has a somewhat typical body form, but there are many variations and unusual forms. The seahorse, for example, doesn't look much like the typical bony fish, even though it belongs to that class.

Often, a fish's shape suits its way of life—or the other way around. The flattened shape of the skates and rays is ideal for lying on the ocean bottom or gliding along just above it, although many skates and rays also swim through the open water. Fish that pursue their prey at high speeds, such as the tuna, have streamlined, torpedo-shaped bodies. The cowfish eats by pecking with its hard, beaklike mouth at the growths on corals and rocks, while the bullhead uses the tentacles around its mouth (called barbels) to probe the mud for worms and other prey. The lumpfish spends most of its time clinging to rocks. Its round shape and pebbled skin blend into the background, to avoid catching a predator's eye.

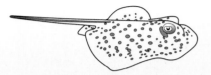

skate

bullhead

tuna

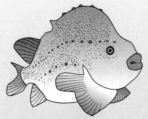

lumpfish

cowfish

seahorse

Illustrations not to scale.

The openings in front of this great white shark's fin are its gill slits. After water has entered the fish's body through its mouth and passed across its gills (which absorb oxygen from the water), it flows out of the body through these slits.

Like all other living things, fish need oxygen, and they have developed a number of ways to get it into their systems. Gills are the primary organ of respiration, or breathing. A gill is a sheet of tissue with very thin cell walls, filled with blood vessels, and usually covered with small folds to increase the surface area. Water is drawn into the fish's body through the mouth. As it flows over the gills, a gas exchange takes place through the thin cell walls. Oxygen leaves the water and enters the blood. At the same time, carbon dioxide, a waste product, leaves the blood to be carried away in the water.

Gills aren't always enough. There is a lot less oxygen in water than in air, and the oxygen content of water varies from place to place. Stagnant water, for example, contains less oxygen than fast-moving water. So while all fish get oxygen from the water through their gills, species that live in low-oxygen waters—swamps, sluggish rivers, and deep lakes—also get oxygen directly from the air, rising to the surface to inhale through their mouths. A few species will die without regular breaths of air. Some air breathers, such as tarpon, mudfishes, bowfin, and lungfishes, have swim bladders that are lungs. Others have tissues for gas exchange in their throats or intestines. Air breathing is just one of the ways that fish have adapted to life in a wide range of environments.

Diplomystus, a fish that lived about 50 million years ago, was a distant relative of modern herrings and sardines. Many *Diplomystus* fossils have been found in the Green River area of Wyoming.

Half a Billion Years of Fish

Fishes were the first creatures to develop skeletons. They were the ancestors of all other animals with skeletons, including human beings. But while one group of ancient fishes developed limbs and migrated onto land to continue their evolution there, most fishes remained in the sea, developing into many families and countless species.

Paleontologists, scientists who study ancient life from fossils and other remains, know that fishes have been around for about 500 million years, or half a billion years. Over that long span, many families of fish appeared, flourished for a time, and then became extinct. The fish that are alive today are descended from just a few of those families. The fossil record of fish evolution is full of holes, but paleontologists are working to piece together the relationships between today's fish families and the ancient families that died out. At the same time, the DNA of living fish is giving ichthyologists new clues about the classification of modern species.

The free-swimming larvae of sea creatures similar to this tunicate may have been the ancestors of the first fishes.

THE FIRST FISHES

During the Cambrian period of Earth's history, which began around 540 million years ago and lasted until 500 million years ago, the seas were full of invertebrates. These were animals without bones, like the sponges, worms, and sea cucumbers of today.

Most scientists think that fish evolved from ancient creatures much like the modern sea animals called tunicates, or sea squirts. Adult tunicates spend their lives attached to the sea bottom, but their larvae, or young, are active and free-swimming until they choose a spot and fasten themselves permanently. The larvae possess spinal nerves and protective notochords, the beginnings of backbones.

According to one widely accepted theory about the origins of vertebrate animals, it all started with ancient larvae. In some species, the larval stage of the life cycle kept getting longer and longer. Eventually the larvae developed the ability to breed without entering the adult stage at all. This paved the way for the appearance of fishes.

The sea once rolled over an area that is now called Chengjiang, in China's Kunming Province. In the 1990s, paleontologists working in Chengjiang unearthed fossils of creatures that died in that long-ago sea and were buried by the mud and sand on its floor. Among them are the fossils of fish in a genus called *Haikouichthys*.

The *Haikouichthys* animals had dorsal fins, heads that looked like the heads on modern lamprey larvae, and folds of skin along their undersides that may be the beginnings of pelvic fins. (One idea about fins is that they evolved from folds or flaps of skin.) There are also signs that they had notochords. At 530 million years old, the *Haikouichthys* fossils are the first known fishes—for now. New fossil finds may push the dawn of fishes still further into the past.

The Chengjiang fossil fishes probably looked like modern hagfishes and lampreys. They didn't have jaws, bony skeletons, or scales. By the end of the Cambrian period, though, fish were developing bones, as well as the bony plates that were the forerunners of scales. Five-hundred-million-year-old fossils of a fish called *Anatolepsis*, which was armored with the bony plates, have been found in several parts of the world. Another armored fish, *Sacabambaspis*, lived 470 million years ago in what is now Bolivia, in South America.

EVOLUTION AND EXTINCTION

Between 500 and 300 million years ago, the ancestral fishes evolved into a multitude of forms. The first to develop were the agnathans, from the Greek words for "without jaws." (Some taxonomists use the term cyclostomes for the jawless fishes.)

Many agnathans had bony armor plates. But like modern hagfishes and lampreys, the agnathans lacked bony jaws that open and close as a pair. Their head shields were made of bone, but their mouths were made of soft tissue. Some mouths were tubes, perhaps for sucking up food from the ocean floor. Others were suction disks. The fish probably used these to fasten on to other fish and suck their blood, as modern lampreys do. Still other early agnathans had mouths adapted for scooping or straining food out of the water.

Several important evolutionary steps appeared in agnathan fishes. Some groups evolved scales and fins. Fossils of a few families show

One of the first jawed fishes was *Dunkleosteus,* which lived around 360 million years ago. It was a placoderm—an armored fish—covered with heavy bone plates. At lengths of up to 20 feet (6 m), armed with sharp bone blades in place of teeth, *Dunkleosteus* was a formidable predator.

evidence of bony toothlike growths. One group of jawless fishes, the thelodonts, had stomachs—a feature not found in the earliest agnathans (or in modern lampreys).

Around 355 million years ago, the Devonian period drew to a close. The agnathans had flourished for millions of years, but the end of the Devonian brought "the end of the jawless empire," as paleontologist and ichthyologist John A. Long puts it in *The Rise of Fishes: 500 Million Years of Evolution* (1995). Almost all of the agnathans became extinct. Just two groups of jawless fishes remained in existence: the myxiniforms and the petromyzontiforms. Scientists think that these two groups arose and evolved separately.

Some paleontologists think that the main reason the jawless fishes disappeared is that they were outcompeted by another group of fishes that had been evolving alongside them. These were the jawed fishes, which may have moved faster or been better at catching prey and defending themselves than the agnathans.

Scientists call the jawed fishes gnathostomes (from the Greek for "having jaws"). The first gnathostomes evolved from one line of agnathan fishes just a few million years after the first agnathans appeared. By the time the agnathans disappeared millions of years later, the gnathostomes had branched out into many new forms.

The first gnathostomes—the oldest jawed fishes—were the acanthodians. Dating from about 440 million years ago, they were generally less than about 8 inches (20 centimeters) long, with large eyes, streamlined bodies covered with bony scales, and spines in front of their fins. The acanthodians survived for about 200 million years before dying out. No living fishes are descended from them.

Another early group of jawed fishes, the placoderms, appeared about 420 million years ago. From the fossil record, it seems that the placoderms were more numerous, and had more species, than the acanthodians. Placoderms were heavily armored with overlapping plates. Some had bony tubes, almost like jointed arm bones, around their pectoral fins. They also had bony teeth. Their internal skeletons seem to have been made of a mixture of cartilage and bone.

The placoderms were very diverse. Among them were the world's first really large animals. *Gorgonichthys,* for example, was almost 20 feet (6 m) long, with powerful jaws and huge, beaklike teeth for catching and crushing prey. The placoderms dominated the oceans for sixty million years, but in spite of their diversity, they didn't last as long as the acanthodians. Placoderms died out at the end of the Devonian period.

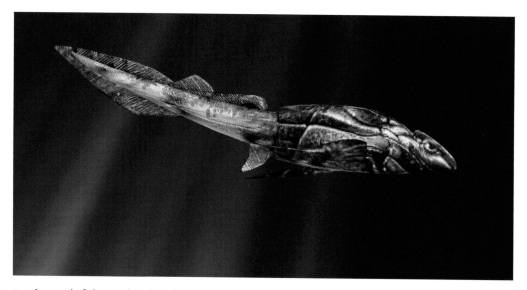

Another early fish was the placoderm *Bothriolepis*, which lived in deep freshwater lakes. It had gills, but two pouches off its throat may have been an early form of lungs. Some paleontologists think *Bothriolepis* could have been an air-breathing fish. This computer image is based on fossil records.

By the time the placoderms and the acanthodians vanished, two other major groups of jawed fishes had established themselves in the seas. One group was the cartilaginous fishes, called chondrichthyans. They first appeared around 400 hundred million years ago, when early sharks evolved. The second group was the bony fishes, or osteichthyans. Both the cartilaginous and the bony fishes were more successful, in evolutionary terms, than the placoderms, acanthodians, and agnathans. Although many species and families that descended from the early chondrichthyans and osteichthyans have disappeared, others have survived. They are the cartilaginous and bony fishes of the modern world.

Along the way, one group of bony fishes gave rise to a new kind of animal that scientists call a tetrapod, meaning "four legs." Tetrapods were the first creatures to walk on legs and to leave the water for the land. They appeared around 375 million years ago and evolved into amphibians, reptiles, birds, and eventually mammals—all of which are tetrapods.

For a long time, scientists knew that the first tetrapods had evolved from fish. Some stages in the process, though, were a mystery. In 2005, paleontologists filled in one of the missing pieces when they found the fossil of a "fishapod," an animal between a fish and a tetrapod.

Called *Tiktaalik roseae*, the fishapod had gills, scales, and other fish features, but it also had features found in tetrapods. Lungs were one such feature. More important was the structure of the fins, which were adapted to hold the fishapod's weight, with sturdy wrist and shoulder bones. Scientists think that *Tiktaalik* and animals like it pushed their way through shallow, marshy waters, raising their crocodile-like heads above water to look around, breathing through both gills and lungs.

Tiktaalik and its kin became extinct long ago, but not before they had evolved into true tetrapods. The descendants of the tetrapods still live on

The "prince of Miguasha" is an ancient, extinct lobe-finned fish, *Eustenopteron foordi*. The nickname comes from the fact that fossils were found in Miguasha, part of Quebec, Canada. Lobe-finned fishes like *E. foordi* eventually gave rise to the tetrapods, the ancestors of land animals.

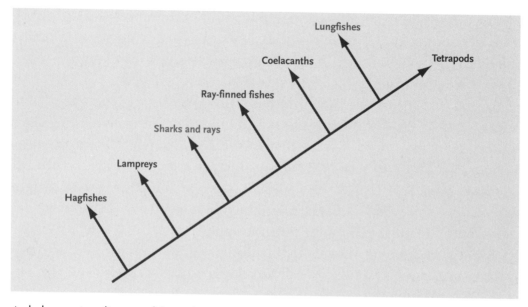

A cladogram is a diagram of the evolutionary relationships among different organisms. The two lines that branch off from any junction lead to sister groups. This cladogram shows that the lungfishes are a sister group to the tetrapods—the category that includes all amphibians, reptiles, birds, and mammals, including human beings.

land—except for the whales and other mammals that returned to the sea. But while tetrapods went their way on land, the fishes remained in the water, continuing their own evolutionary path to the present.

The Fish That Time Forgot

Soon after the fishing vessel *Nerine* docked in the South African city of East London, a visitor came aboard. Her name was Marjorie Courtenay-Latimer, and she ran a small local museum. The captain of the *Nerine* often gave her interesting items from his catch so that she could display them in the museum. On this December afternoon in 1938, Courtenay-Latimer was about to find the most extraordinary fish ever caught by the *Nerine*.

She noticed a glimmering blue fin beneath a pile of starfish, small sharks, and other familiar sea creatures. The fin turned out to belong to what she called "the most beautiful fish I had ever seen." About 5 feet (1.5 m) long, it was covered with hard spiny scales in shades of blue, green, red, and brown, spotted with white. Its fins were thick and fleshy, and its tail fin was unlike anything Courtenay-Latimer knew. A small secondary fin extended from it, like a miniature tail at the end of the larger tail.

Courtenay-Latimer wrapped the fish in a sack and had it loaded into the trunk of her taxi (whose driver deserves credit for hauling a big dead fish in the service of science). Back at the museum, she tried to identify the unusual specimen, but she couldn't find it in any of her reference books. Then she remembered reading that fossils of ancient fish revealed stiff scales with spines, just like the ones on her mystery fish. Some ancient fishes had also had fleshy fins called lobe fins. Could the mystery fish be related to those long-vanished creatures? She wrote to an ichthyologist named J.L.B. Smith for help.

As soon as Smith saw Courtenay-Latimer's careful drawing of her find, he was sure it was a coelacanth, a fish that scientists knew only through fossils. Coelacanths appeared in the fossil record about 400 million years ago, but the youngest coelacanth fossils ever found were about 70 million years old. Everyone thought that coelacanths had been extinct since before the dinosaurs disappeared. Finding a fresh specimen would be one of the scientific marvels of the century.

Examination of Courtenay-Latimer's specimen proved that it was a coelacanth. It was given the scientific name *Latimeria chalumnae*. The genus name honors its discoverer, and the species name refers to the Chalumna River, because the fish was caught at sea near the river's mouth.

The coelacanth was a worldwide sensation, a fossil that had come to life. Smith and other scientists were determined to learn more about this astonishing survival. The first step was to find more specimens. World War II interfered with the search, and it wasn't until 1952 that another coelacanth came to light. It was caught in the Comoro Islands, in the Indian Ocean close to the African coast. Within two years, five more coelacanths

"A living fossil," the coelacanth was thought to have become extinct 65 million years ago—until fishermen netted a specimen in 1938. This coelacanth was caught off the coast of Kenya in 2001.

had been netted in the Comoros, and by the late 1980s, scientists had studied nearly two hundred specimens. Some of these fish were alive when brought to the surface, but they all died within a few hours, in spite of many attempts to keep them alive. The journey to the surface seemed to be fatal to coelacanths. The next step would be to observe live coelacanths in their natural habitat.

The first such sighting took place from a submersible (a small research submarine) in 1987. Since that time, scientists have filmed many hours of coelacanth activity from submersibles. They now know that the four fins on a coelacanth's underside—two in front and two in the rear—are highly flexible. When the coelacanth swims, it moves these two pairs of fins in the same way that reptiles move their legs when they walk: the right front and left rear move at the same time, then the left front and right rear. No other fish moves its fins in this way. Scientists also learned, by studying a pregnant female specimen, that coelacanths give birth to live young.

A second species of coelacanth was identified in 1997 in Indonesia. Some ichthyologists believe that other coelacanth species may wait to be discovered elsewhere in the Indian Ocean, or beyond it.

Since 2000, dive teams have been swimming with coelacanths, and filming them. Their goal is to locate pups, the young of the coelacanth. If pups can be fitted with radiotransmitter tags, scientists will be able to monitor their movements. This might answer some questions about these ancient creatures: Where do they spend most of their time? What are the stages of their life cycle? How long do they live? And, just possibly, coelacanths might lead researchers to other undiscovered species. After all, the coelacanth went unnoticed by science until 1938. Other surprises could be hidden in the ocean's depths.

Scientists in research submarines have filmed the coelacanth in its natural habitat, the rocky seabeds and underwater caves of the Indo-Pacific region.

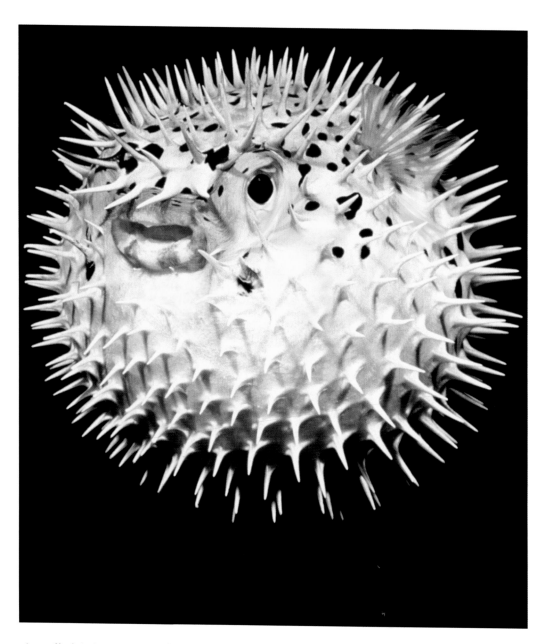

The pufferfish doesn't always look like this. When threatened, pufferfish swallow water or air to inflate themselves until they appear several times their usual size.

With and Without Jaws

Fish classification should probably be written in pencil, because it changes often. Scientists have a lot of unanswered questions about relationships among ancient and modern groups of fishes. Another way of putting it is that scientists have many answers to those questions but do not agree on which answers are correct.

No taxonomic scheme for fishes is accepted by all ichthyologists. Many experts, however, follow the system published by Joseph S. Nelson in *Fishes of the World* (2006). It recognizes 515 families of fishes, grouped into 62 orders. The orders are collected into five classes. Two of the classes are jawless fishes. Three are jawed fishes. Of the jawed fishes, one class is cartilaginous and two are bony.

JAWLESS FISHES

Jawless fishes are divided into two main groups, the hagfishes and the lampreys. Hagfishes don't look much like the typical image of a fish. Even Linnaeus, the father of taxonomy, mistakenly thought they were worms.

The Pacific hagfish belongs to one of the two surviving groups of jawless fishes. This one was photographed off Monterey, California.

They have thick skin that covers their eyes, skeletons made completely of cartilage, and long, narrow bodies with no paired fins. Fleshy, tentacle-like sense organs called barbels around their mouths help them detect food. Hagfishes are bottom dwellers that live in burrows and prey on small animals such as worms. They also scavenge on dead or dying fish. The seventy or so existing species of hagfishes belong to the class Myxini.

The lampreys are similar to the hagfishes in body structure. Like the hagfishes, they come in many sizes, with the largest more than 3.3 feet (1 m) in length. There are around thirty-eight known species of lamprey. They belong to the class Petromyzontida.

All lampreys are born in fresh water. They spend much of their lives as larvae, living in stream bottoms and feeding on microscopic animals. Once they take on their adult forms, the smaller species stop eating. They die soon after breeding and rarely venture far from their area where they were born.

Larger lamprey species migrate out to sea or to large lakes, where they prey on living fish (and sometimes mammals). Using their round mouths like suction cups, they fasten themselves to their prey, gnaw into the body with rasping toothlike structures made of horn, and drink blood or other body fluids. Lampreys that are smaller than their hosts often do not kill the hosts; they move on to fresh prey, leaving the hosts weakened but alive. Some lampreys, however, prey on fish close to their own size, or suck out the host's internal organs. In these cases, the hosts die.

Instead of jaws, lampreys have round, toothed mouths that they use as suction devices. They attach themselves to other fish, chew into their hosts' bodies, and start eating.

CARTILAGINOUS FISHES

The class Chondrichthyes includes about 970 species of fishes that have jaws and also have skeletons that are made of cartilage, not bone. Cartilaginous fishes never have swim bladders. The males of all species have pelvic fins that have evolved into "claspers" for gripping the female's body during mating. The scales of cartilaginous fishes are hard, toothlike structures that sit on top of the skin. These placoid scales, as they are called, give the skin a rough surface, like sandpaper.

The tiger shark, like all sharks and many other kinds of fishes, has a skeleton that is made of a dense, tough, slightly rubbery tissue called cartilage—similar to the material of a human ear.

Divers encounter a giant manta ray, *Manta birostris*, at a marine sanctuary off the coast of Louisiana.

The great majority of cartilaginous fishes are elasmobranchs, a subclass that includes sharks, skates, and rays. Nearly all elasmobranchs are marine creatures, but a few species of sharks and rays live in fresh water, or at least enter it from time to time. Sharks typically have a torpedo-shaped body. Many species are large, although full-grown dwarf sharks are often less than 8 inches (20 cm) in length. Skates and rays have flat bodies with long, narrow tails and flat fins that look like wings on either side. The largest of these species is the manta ray, which can be more than 23 feet (7 m) across.

TWO TYPES OF FISH

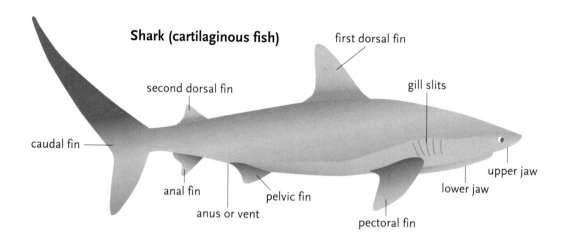

Shark (cartilaginous fish)

first dorsal fin

second dorsal fin

gill slits

caudal fin

anal fin

pelvic fin

upper jaw

anus or vent

lower jaw

pectoral fin

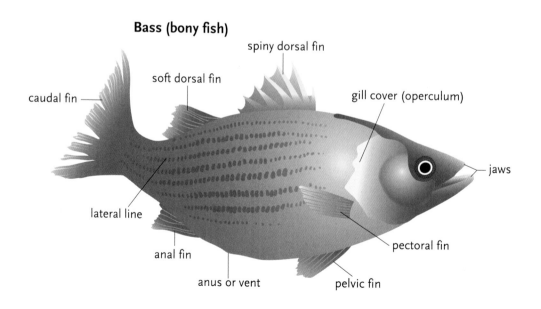

Bass (bony fish)

spiny dorsal fin

soft dorsal fin

caudal fin

gill cover (operculum)

jaws

lateral line

anal fin

pectoral fin

anus or vent

pelvic fin

The New Zealand elephantfish belongs to a group of cartilaginous fishes called the chimaeras, after mythical Greek beasts that combined the features of multiple animals. The name elephantfish refers to the fish's long snout. This species is harvested commercially around Australia and New Zealand.

Thirty-one species of cartilaginous fishes fall into a second subclass, the holocephalans. These fishes have also been called chimaeras, after a mythological creature that combined the features of two or more animals. The holocephalans have long, narrow bodies, with large heads that remind some people of other kinds of animals. Common names for these fishes include rabbitfish, ratfish, and elephantfish.

Holocephalans have a single gill slit on each side of the body, but they also take in water through their nostrils for breathing, something no other class of fish does. They have poisonous spines in front of their dorsal fins for defense. Males have fleshy growths on their foreheads and near their pelvic fins. No one is sure what purpose these growths serve, but because they are found only on males, they are probably used in mating. The teeth of holocephalans are large and flat, perfect for crushing hard foods such as the clams and lobsters that the fish find as they hunt on the sea bottom. A few species live in shallow water near land, but most of these rarely seen creatures live in deep water.

The harlequin ghost pipefish, like its relatives the seahorses, has scales that form a stiff, boxy case around the body. Seen in isolation, the fish looks gaudy, but it spends most of its time near coral growths. Its spines, skin flaps, and elaborate coloration help it blend into the surrounding coral.

BONY FISHES

The bony fishes are by far the largest group of fishes today, with about 27,000 species. Some experts think that that number will go up, because thousands of additional species have not yet been identified! Right now, though, the bony fishes account for half of all known species of animals with backbones.

Bony fishes have skeletons made of bone, or a combination of bone and cartilage. Another feature of nearly all bony fishes is the operculum, a flap that covers the gill slits (the gill slits of cartilaginous fishes are uncovered). Many bony fishes also have swim bladders.

The scales of bony fishes are different from the toothlike, placoid scales of the cartilaginous fishes. In general, bony fishes have ctenoid scales. These are thin, overlapping plates of bone set in pockets of skin, but there is great variety. In boxfishes, pipefishes, and seahorses, for example, the scales are fused together to form a stiff case around the body. Sticklebacks and shrimp fishes are armored in tough plates, while catfishes and some other groups have no scales at all.

The bony fishes are divided into two classes: Sarcopterygii and Actinopterygii.

Lobe-finned Fishes

The Sarcopterygii are called lobe-finned fishes, or flesh-finned fishes, because their fins are not flat bundles of rays like the fins of other bony fish. Instead, sarcopterygian fishes have flexible fins that are like stubby limbs. They consist of sections, or lobes, of flesh over internal skeletons. Often, these lobes have rayed edges.

Tetrapods evolved from sarcopterygians hundreds of millions of years ago. Today, only eight species of sarcopterygians are known to exist. Two of them are coelacanths, deepwater fish that scientists thought had died out about 70 million years ago—until live coelacanths were discovered in the twentieth century. The two species of coelacanths live in the tropical Indo-Pacific region.

African lungfishes like this one can breathe air through their lungs. When the pools where they live dry up, they seal themselves into burrows and wait—for several years, if necessary—for rainfall to renew the pools.

Tarpon, large game fish sought after by sport fishers, have some features in common with ancient, ancestral fishes.

The other six species of sarcopterygians are lungfishes. They live in freshwater habitats such as muddy pools and swamps, where the water is poor in oxygen, and they have highly efficient lungs for breathing air. One species of lungfish is native to South America, one to Australia, and four to Africa. The African and American lungfishes have long, flexible, small-scaled bodies and fins like threads or tentacles. The Australian species has flipperlike fins, larger scales, and a taller body. It looks more like the fossils of ancient lungfishes than the other modern species do.

African lungfishes have evolved a way of surviving dry seasons, when the waters dry up. Before the water is gone, they squirm into the mud, forming water-filled burrows. Then they release a mucus from their bodies that hardens, sealing the fish inside the burrow. A narrow tube with a mud plug connects the inside of the burrow to the surface. Once the fish is sealed into its burrow, it enters a state called estivation, which requires very little oxygen. The fish lives by digesting the tissues of its own body for as long as four years, until rain comes and dissolves the plug. Water passes through the tube and into the burrow, waking the fish.

Ray-finned Fishes

The Actinopterygii are called ray-finned fishes because their fins are thin membranes supported by frameworks of ribs, or rays. The rays may be either spiny and stiff or soft and flexible. Some fishes have both types.

In general, fish with only soft rays have features that ichthyologists call ancestral, meaning that they closely resemble features seen in fossil fishes. Soft-rayed fishes include bony-tongues, gars, eels, tarpons, and herrings. Spiny-rayed fishes have more derived features, which means that they are further removed from the earlier forms. Lanternfishes, flyingfishes, perches, basses, and scorpionfishes are examples of spiny-rayed families.

Flyingfishes don't really fly—but they do leap out of the water and glide above the surface with their fins spread wide like wings. This ability gives the fifty or so species of flyingfishes an edge when it comes to escaping from predators such as tuna.

The American paddlefish, *Polyodon spathula*, lives in the Mississippi River and other large, slow-moving rivers that empty into it. Its species name, *spathula*, is a Latin word for "blade"—and also the source for the name of a common kitchen utensil.

The actinoptergyian fishes fall into two subclasses. One subclass, Chondrostei, contains fishes that somewhat resembles the members of other groups: the lungfishes, the coelacanths, and even the cartilaginous fishes. For example, bichirs and reedfishes, which are found in Africa, have lobed, fleshy pectoral fins like coelacanths. Bichirs also have lungs for breathing air, something not found in the majority of ray-finned fishes.

The subclass Chondrostei also includes the sturgeons and paddlefishes. These have cartilaginous skeletons, even though they fall within the category of bony fishes. Their upper jaws don't move separately from their heads, even though they are considered jawed fishes.

There are twenty-five species of sturgeons and two of paddlefishes. All of them are found in rivers in North America, Europe, and northern Asia, although some species of sturgeons spend part of their lives in salt water. Sturgeons often make long journeys up rivers to breed. Beluga sturgeons (whose eggs are eaten as the delicacy caviar) once traveled as much as 2,000 miles (4,000 kilometers) from the Black and Caspian seas up Europe's Danube and Volga rivers. Dams and locks on the rivers have ended these epic journeys, though, and the surviving populations of beluga sturgeons make shorter migrations.

The beluga sturgeons are the largest fish ever found in fresh water. They have been reported to reach lengths of almost 30 feet (9 m) and weights of 3,300 pounds (1,500 kilograms). These and other large sturgeons, though,

The largest fish found in fresh waters is the Beluga sturgeon, which is now endangered. These fish, however, spend part of their lives in salt water.

INTERNAL ANATOMY

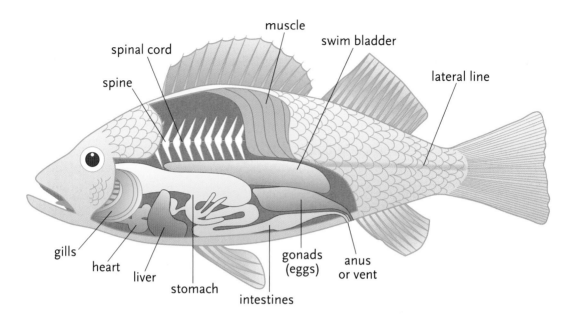

spend part of their lives in salt water. The largest full-time freshwater fish species may be *Pangasianodon gigas,* the Mekong giant catfish, found in the Mekong River of Southeast Asia. In 2005, fishermen in Thailand caught one of these catfish that was 9 feet (2.7 m) long and weighed 646 pounds (293 kg). Some researchers think that even larger freshwater specimens may exist among the Chinese paddlefish, the South American arapaima (also called the pirarucu), or the giant Mekong stringray.

The second subclass of ray-finned fishes is the Neopterygii, which means "new fins." Some ichthyologists divide the neopterygian fishes into two groups. One group is small, containing just the bowfin and the garfishes. The muscle and nerve structure that supports their rayed tail fins is different from that found in the teleosts, as rest of the neopterygians are sometimes called. The teleosts far outnumber all the other groups of fishes. About 96 percent of the fish species in the world are teleosts.

Body shapes and physical features vary wildly among the teleosts, and so do their habitats and ways of life. Fishes that live in steep, fast-flowing streams, for example, have evolved mechanisms for anchoring themselves so that they are not swept away. Catfishes and carps cling to surfaces with their enlarged lips. Hillside loaches use their paired pectoral or pelvic fins, together with their bellies, to form "suction cups" that fasten them in place.

Cave-dwelling freshwater fishes that live in darkness have become blind, or partly blind, because their eyes are useless. Their lateral-line sensory systems, however, are enlarged. This helps them "feel" the surroundings they cannot see.

A Mexican blind cavefish is one of many freshwater species that have lost their eyesight—and their eyes—because they do not need to see in their dark environments.

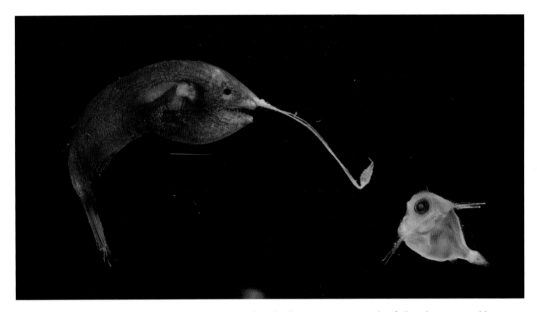

An anglerfish, a deep-sea dweller, lures prey with a bioluminescent growth of skin that moves like a tiny fish. When another fish tries to eat the lure, it gets eaten by the anglerfish.

Fishes that dwell in the eternal darkness of the deep sea have lights built into their bodies, in the form of organs made up of cells called photophores. The photophores produce light in one of two ways: through chemical reactions inside the cells or, less often, through the actions of glowing bacteria that live in the cells. Lanternfishes, dragonfishes, and deep-sea anglerfishes are well-known luminescent, or light-producing, fishes, but about two-thirds of all deep-sea species have some degree of luminescence. Light seems to have many uses, such as signaling to members of the same species and luring prey within reach. Fish may also use their lights to startle predators, hoping to escape in the confusion.

Of all the teleosts, the longest may be the oarfish, with a maximum length of 36.3 feet (11 m). The world's shortest fishes, both freshwater and marine, are teleosts. Minnows, members of the genus *Phoxinus*, are the shortest freshwater fishes. The smallest marine species, the Philippine goby, is even tinier. Adults of that species may be just 0.33 inch (0.8 cm) long.

Teleosts are remarkably diverse in habitats as well as size. Families and species have adapted to life everywhere in the water, from mudflats and tide pools to oceanic abysses, from the mineral-rich waters of desert hot springs to the cold realm under the Antarctic ice.

Shrimp gobies are fish that live in symbiosis with shrimp. The arrangement benefits both partners— the shrimp digs a burrow that both creatures share, while the goby uses its superior eyesight to protect the shrimp from predators. When the shrimp is outside the burrow, it keeps one antenna on the fish's tailfin. If the goby senses danger, it flicks its tail to send a warning signal to the shrimp, which then scuttles back to safety.

Gentle Giants of the Sea

"A whale of a shark!" is how one swimmer at Australia's Ningaloo Reef described the largest known species of living fish: *Rhincodon typus,* the whale shark. Its common name is a little confusing, because the fish is a shark, not a whale (whales are mammals).

But the whale shark does have something in common with the blue whale, the world's largest animal. Both are filter feeders. They cruise through the sea with their huge mouths wide open. At back of the whale shark's mouth, the water passes through gill plates, which are structures like filters. The plates catch food items—small fishes, fish eggs, little shrimps, and the tiny creatures known as krill and plankton—and filter them into the shark's digestive system. The water passes through the plates, across the gills, and back out into the sea through the gill slits. The whale shark is one of just three filter-feeding sharks (the others are the megamouth and the basking shark).

Reaching lengths of up to 50 feet (15 m), whale sharks are slow-moving and unaggressive. They are found in the waters of more than a hundred nations, usually swimming near the surface. This lets snorkelers, divers, and tour boats get close to these mighty fish, but it also puts the whale sharks at high risk of being captured in fishing nets or colliding with boats.

The world population of whale sharks is unknown, but most scientists who have studied these fish fear that their number is declining. Since 2000, the World Conservation Union has identified whale sharks as vulnerable to extinction, partly because of overfishing as food—their flesh is considered a delicacy in parts of Asia. Several nations have outlawed the hunting of these enormous, peaceful animals. One country, the

Philippines, is trying to preserve whale sharks while saving the economies of communities that once fished for them. These whale-fishing centers have become tourist spots, where visitors have a chance to swim with the protected giants of the sea.

The majestic whale shark is the largest living fish.

An archerfish squirts a precisely aimed jet of water to knock an insect from its perch. An instant later it will gobble up the fallen bug.

The Fish's Life

"Master, I marvel how the fishes live in the sea," says a fisherman in the second act of William Shakespeare's play *Pericles.* Another fisherman replies that fishes live in the sea in the same way that people live on land—"the great ones eat up the little ones."

Shakespeare was only partly right. Most fishes do live by feeding on smaller species. Or on bigger ones, as when a school of piranhas strips the flesh from a catfish, or a hagfish enters the mouth of a cod and devours it from the inside. But the eating habits of fishes, like everything else about them, are very diverse. People are learning more about the fishes, and finding new species of them, all the time. Some of the people studying fish hope to use their knowledge to preserve this group of animals, whose roots go so far back into the past.

FEEDING

Some fishes eat almost anything. Cichlids in African lakes, for example, feed on whatever they can get, from microscopic plant matter to other fish, or even scales pulled off other fish. At the other extreme, some species are

The powerful teeth and heavy protective scales of the titan triggerfish allow it to feast on the long-spined sea urchin. Found on reefs in tropical Pacific and Asian waters, these territorial triggerfish have been known to nip at divers viewed as intruders.

picky eaters, with diets that are limited to a few items, or only one. Some Amazon catfishes, for example, drink blood from larger fish. They get the blood by swimming into the bigger fishes' gills to live. They suck the blood through the thin tissues of the hosts' gill walls.

The cichlids are omnivores, fish that eat both plant and animal foods. Other omnivores include carp, catfishes, and some trout. Some fishes have been called herbivores, or plant eaters, because they graze on algae and aquatic weeds. However, these fishes probably also eat the microscopic animals, insects, small snails, shrimps, and other creatures that live in the plants. And even fishes that eat mostly plant foods when they are adults survive their larval stages by eating tiny creatures, such as the drifting animals called zooplankton.

The great majority of fishes are carnivores, or meat eaters. The bulk of their diet consists of worms, shrimps and their relatives, water-dwelling insects or insect larvae, clams, and young fish—including, in many cases, the young of their own species. Many fish that live near the surface in fresh water feed on insects and insect larvae that fall into the water. Some don't wait for their prey to fall. The archerfish of tropical Asia is one of several kind of fish that knock bugs out of the air by spitting jets of water at them.

The pale growth in front of this warty frogfish's eye extends a lure that may draw a hungry, unsuspecting fish within reach of the frogfish's wide, downturned mouth. These fish are sometimes seen moving slowly across the bottom by "walking" on their fins.

Large predators of the open ocean, such as the tunas and sharks, can cover great distances on feeding migrations as they hunt for prey. A lot of bottom-dwelling species follow a different strategy: they lie in wait for a meal to pass by. Some groups, such as the viperfishes and frogfishes, have growths on their heads that look like small prey animals. Dangled in front of the lurking fish's mouth, the growth acts as a lure. A fish swims toward the lure, thinking that it has spotted a meal . . . and suddenly the waiting predator strikes.

BREEDING

All fish breed sexually, which means that male and female sex cells join to produce the fertilized eggs that will become the next generation. Fish have several ways of getting the male and female cells together. All cartilaginous fishes, and some bony fishes, mate. The male inserts sperm into the female's body, where it fertilizes her eggs. Afterward, the female lays the eggs, or, in many species of sharks and rays, she gives birth to live young.

Another method of getting sperm and eggs together is spawning. Most teleosts reproduce this way. Spawning occurs when male fish deposit sperm and female fish deposit eggs directly into the water. This may take place at a spawning territory or over a nest, such as a small pit in the ocean or stream floor, a circle of pebbles, or a cluster of vegetation. The male parent usually prepares the nest to attract females. Studies of fish behavior suggest that most species perform some kind of courtship behavior before spawning. One or both partners may change color or "dance."

Parental care ranges from none to some. Fishes are not particularly nurturing parents. One group of researchers estimated that 78 percent of teleost species give no parental care at all. Both parents simply swim away after depositing their genetic material in the water. In 11 percent of species, the male parent tends the eggs or young; in 7 percent the female is the caretaker; and in 4 percent the two share the job. Caretaking duties include keeping

Salmon leap up a waterfall in southeastern Alaska. They return to where they were born in order to have their own breeding season.

Grunion are among the very few fishes that spawn on land. They arrive by night, at the same time each year, to lay their eggs in the wet sand of some southern California beaches.

the eggs clean and driving predators away from eggs (and, in some species, from the young). A protective parents usually stands guard over the nest, but sometimes the parent carries the eggs. Male seahorses and pipefishes keep fertilized eggs in pouches on their bellies. Cardinalfishes, jawfishes, and some others carry them in pouches inside their mouths.

Species that give parental care generally produce fewer fertilized eggs than those that give no care, but they invest time and energy to improve the eggs' chances of survival. Species that provide no care are leaving the survival of their eggs up to chance, but they may produce millions of eggs in a single spawning. Even if a great many eggs are eaten by predators, the odds are good that a few will make it.

The life cycles of fishes are as variable as their breeding and parenting methods. Cartilaginous fishes give birth to highly developed young that look like small versions of their parents. These young fishes simply get

Among seahorses, the males become pregnant and give birth to the young. This male seahorse has just released his tiny offspring from his brood pouch.

bigger until they have reached their adult size. Most young bony fishes in saltwater environments have a different form than their parents. They hatch from their eggs as larvae, and they may spend a large percentage of their lives in the larval stage, before taking their adult forms. Freshwater fishes are less likely to have a recognizable or prolonged larval stage. Many species hatch as miniature versions of adults.

The larva of a deep-sea anglerfish in enclosed in what remains of its large, yolky egg. This egg provides protection and nutrition for the young fish as it develops on its own in the cold, challenging environment.

SOCIAL RELATIONSHIPS

Some fishes are solitary, except when spawning, but many have social relationships. Such a relationship may consist of nothing more than a fish accepting another's presence, living and feeding in the same area without attacking the other. At other times, though, fish deliberately interact with one another.

One-on-one relationships can exist between fish of two different species. For example, a small fish such as a pilotfish or remora may accompany a shark so that it can eat scraps from the shark's prey. This is a commensal relationship, which means that it benefits one partner and has no effect on the other.

A small, black-striped cleaner wrasse picks parasites and debris from the red gills of a much larger pufferfish. Wrasses maintain cleaning stations where fish have been seen lined up, waiting for their turn to be groomed.

Sometimes the relationship is a mutual symbiosis, which means that it benefits both sides. Snorkelers near tropical reefs may see a symbiotic relationship in action if they come upon a cleaning station—the reef's version of a skin-care salon. A small fish called a cleaner wrasse positions itself at the station. A fish of another species, perhaps even a large, predatory species such as a barracuda, approaches the wrasse. This "client" fish then holds still while the wrasse carefully nibbles tiny parasites and bits of debris from its skin. The wrasse may even enter the client's gills or mouth.

Cleaning symbiosis is a win-win situation. The client is relieved of uncomfortable or harmful parasites, and the cleaner gets to eat all day without having to look for food. How do fish learn the "rules" of cleaning symbiosis? Ichthyologists don't yet know. They do know, however, that

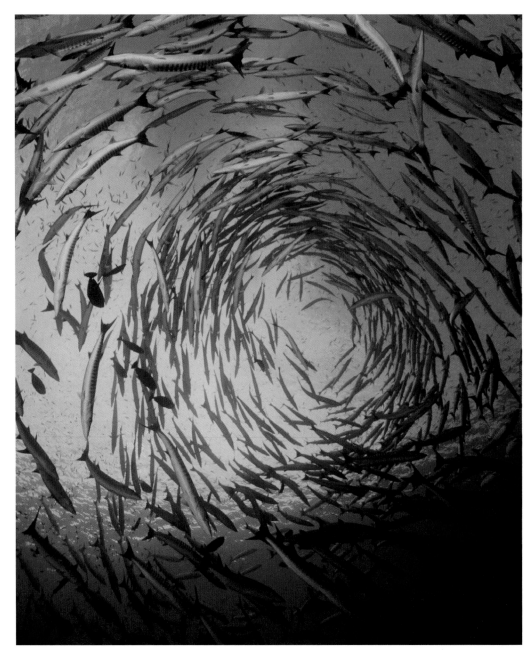

A school of barracuda swims in a tight spiral. Schooling is "strength in numbers" against predators, but schools of fish may also act together to "herd" their own prey into shallow waters for easier hunting.

damselfish that have been raised in the lab from eggs know how to behave like clients when they see a cleaner wrasse for the first time.

When a lot of fish belonging to a single species get together, the result is a shoal or a school. A shoal is a group of fish that have come together for feeding, breeding, or migration. Shoals can be quite densely packed, but each fish acts as an individual, and the gathering may last only a short time.

Schools are longer-lasting and more highly organized than shoals. In a school, the individual fish act like well-coordinated parts of a single large organism. They move together, close but not touching, even during complicated maneuvers such as turning. Schools are not usually made up of fish that are related to one another, and they do not have permanent leaders. The same fish may be a leader at one moment and a follower the next. Researchers have suggested many possible reasons for schooling. Among them are protection from attack by predators, easier movement through the water for a "single" school than for many small fish, and strength in numbers when invading a new feeding territory.

At night, a school is likely to become a shoal. The fish remain together, but they are not moving in a purposeful, coordinated way. They hang in the water in the inactive state that is the fishes' version of sleep. Their eyes are open (fish cannot close their eyes), but the fish are quiet. In the morning, when they become active again, the shoal will tighten formation and return to being a school.

Many fishes are active only by day or only by night. They spend their inactive periods resting quietly in reef crevices, on lake bottoms, or simply drifting. Not all fishes have an inactive period. Tunas, sharks, and some other pelagic fishes remain in constant movement and never "sleep." Cavefishes also remain continuously active.

A diver photographs the scene as giant bluefin tuna are trapped in fishing nets off the coast of Sardinia, Italy. People have been fishing in this spot for more than a thousand years.

Fish and People

Throughout history, people have valued fishes as food resources. High in protein, low in unhealthy fats, fish are a staple food in many Asian and Scandinavian cultures. Fish consumption is on the rise in other cultures, too. In addition to eating fish, people catch them for recreation and sport, collect and observe them in home aquariums, and travel great distances to view them in their natural habitats by diving and snorkeling among them. But in spite of the value we place on fish, humans are now having what ichthyologist Michael Barton, author of *Bond's Biology of Fishes* (2007) calls an "enormous, often devastating impact" on fishes.

Many factors threaten fish populations and species today. Global warming—caused, at least in part, by air pollution and the burning of fossil fuels—will affect fishes along with every other form of life. Other threats are more specific. For example, desert pupfishes that live in springs in Death Valley National Park are losing their habitat to the water-hungry city of Las Vegas, which is draining the underground sources of water that supply the springs.

Habitat loss affects both freshwater and marine fishes. Coral reefs are blown up when fishermen use dynamite to stun their catch, and seafloor

Dead fish litter the banks of China's Songhua river in 2005, after an explosion at a chemical plant raised levels of the toxic substance benzene in the water to more than a hundred times the national safety level.

ecosystems are destroyed by fishing vessels that drag lines or nets across the bottom. Around the world, coastal ecosystems such as swamps, wetlands, and salt marshes are being damaged or filled in as these "useless" areas are turned into airports, marinas, housing developments, and industrial sites. The loss of coastal habitats affects the fishes that spend their lives in these bays, marshes, and lagoons, but it also affects many other species that use these sheltered ecosystems for breeding or seasonal feeding.

Water pollution is another problem that affects fishes in both fresh and salt water. On land, pollutants such as chemicals from fertilizer wash into streams and kill the eggs and larvae of salmon and other fishes. At sea, high levels of toxic pollutants such as mercury and chemical compounds called PCBs build up in the bodies of marine predators, such as tunas and swordfishes, that eat a lot of smaller fish. This accumulation of toxins isn't good for the fish or the people who eat the fish.

Sometimes fishes' biggest problem is other fish—the harmful species that people have introduced to waters where they don't occur naturally. These intruders are called exotic or invasive species. Sometimes they are released on purpose. For example, striped bass were introduced to the Pacific coast of North America in the nineteenth century as sport fish. Now they are threatening native salmon populations.

People also introduce invasive species without realizing it. Ballast water from oceangoing ships, for example, often contains fishes that are emptied into the sea far from their native waters. In recent years an Asian fish called the yellowfin goby has established itself in California. It was probably carried there in ballast water. Now it is competing for food and habitat with rare gobies that are native to California. Another invasive species, a Chinese fish called the northern snakehead, is sold in the United States as an aquarium and food fish. It made headlines in 2002 when it was discovered in lakes in the eastern part of the country. The snakehead is an aggressive predator that could do great damage to native populations of fish and other creatures such as amphibians. Wildlife managers have poisoned entire lakes, killing everything in them, just to control the snakehead threat.

Fishes are being affected by fishing, especially large-scale commercial fishing with high-technology tools for scooping up massive quantities of fish. Industrial fishing affects fish populations in three ways. It removes large numbers of the target species, and it can destroy or damage habitat. But fishing nets and lines also catch—and kill—vast numbers of fish that aren't targeted. Some experts estimate that each year's bycatch, as it is called, is equal to about a third of the commercial fish harvest.

Overfishing has led to dramatic collapses of fish population. Effects of such losses go far beyond the fish themselves. When herring were overfished near Norway in the late twentieth century, for example, populations of sea birds, seals, and cod also plunged, because those animals had lost a key food source. The problem of overfishing is not likely to go away. The United Nations Food and Agriculture Organization has estimated that by 2011, the worldwide demand for seafood will be 50 percent higher than the amount of fish that can be supplied.

The juvenile northern snakehead doesn't look like much of a threat . . . but wait until it grows up. Adult snakeheads introduced into new ecosystems soon devour native fish and other animals.

"Bycatch" is the fishing industry's term for fish, turtles, and sea mammals who are killed in nets or lines that are being used to harvest other species. This hammerhead shark has no hope of freeing itself.

The problems faced by fishes often have more than one cause, and solutions won't be easy. People in the Pacific Northwest, for example, are debating how best to save their native salmon species. The salmon populations have shrunk drastically. Overfishing, dams that block migration routes to spawning sites, and water pollution have likely contributed to the decline. To save the salmon, communities, government, and resource management agencies are trying a combination of steps, including fishing limits and the removal of some small dams. Fishing limits bring hardship to fishermen and communities that depend on the fishing industry, but without strict limits, there may be no fish, and no

A biologist shows volunteers how endangered Chinook salmon will be captured and used to create a breeding population on Idaho's Snake River.

fishing industry, in years to come. Future generations deserve to eat fish—but they also deserve to marvel at the astonishing variety of fishes that share our world.

FIRST TO DISAPPEAR?

Marine fish—species that live in the oceans—can't be wiped out through overfishing. At least, that's what scientists thought for a long time. They believed that the world's seas and oceans are so vast that there would always be places untouched by human activity. Species that declined dramatically as a result of fishing generally bounced back as soon as limits on the catch were enforced. As a result, the idea took hold that marine fish species were "essentially immune to extinction," as ichthyologist Michael Barton puts it in *Bond's Biology of Fishes* (2007).

But many ichthyologists and marine biologists now share a growing fear that species of ocean fish will soon start becoming extinct, something that is already happening to freshwater species. In fact, the first marine species to disappear in modern times may already be gone. Experts disagree about whether marine fish species have become extinct in recent years and, if so, how many are gone. Some believe that several dozen species are already lost. Yet the extinction of a marine species is hard to prove, because it's all but impossible to know for sure that a few survivors aren't alive somewhere in the sea. The clearest case of extinction is one involving a fish with a small geographic range and a habitat that is easier to survey than the open ocean. If no specimens of that fish have been seen for a while, there's a good chance it has gone extinct.

The New Zealand grayling was that kind of fish. Although the young grayling spent several months at sea as part of their life cycle, they spent most of their lives in New Zealand's freshwater rivers and streams. Grayling were harvested for food, so heavily overfished that they disappeared in the mid-twentieth century. As of fall 2006, the New Zealand

The smalltooth sawfish, found in waters off Florida's coast, uses its long, rough-edged snout for catching and killing food. Unfortunately, many sawfish have gotten entangled in fishing lines and nets over the years. The species is now endangered.

grayling was the only marine fish species listed as extinct by the World Conservation Union (IUCN), which monitors the status of species worldwide.

Many other fishes, though, are hanging onto survival by a thread. Sharks and rays are especially at risk, from deliberate overfishing or accidental entanglement in fishing nets or lines. The barndoor skate may be the next victim of extinction. It is a large, slow-moving bottom feeder that is often caught by ships fishing for cod or pollock in the North Atlantic. Habitat destruction is another threat to many species of fish. Building a tropical resort hotel, for example, might involve clearing mangrove forest out of a lagoon, taking away the food and protection of species that breed in the lagoon.

The IUCN lists thirty-three species of marine fish as critically endangered. So far, the saltwater fishes are in better shape than the freshwater species. Eighty-one freshwater species have become extinct in recent years, and another 232 are critically endangered. But some scientists fear what Ellen Pikitch of the Pew Institute for Ocean Science calls "a gathering wave of ocean extinctions."

Are humans to blame for the plight of these species on the brink of extinction? After all, countless species became extinct before humans existed. The problem today is the rate of extinction—it is happening more often than the average "background rate" of extinctions over millions of years. Says Elliott A. Norse of the Marine Conservation Biology Institute, "Extinctions happen in the ocean; the fossil record shows that marine species have disappeared since life began in the sea. The question is, are humans a major new force causing marine extinctions? The evidence, and projections scientists are making, suggest that the answer is yes." Yet if humans are causing the problem, then they also have the power to solve it. Measures such as fishery-free zones and severe penalties for overfishing may save some of the endangered marine fishes from plunging over the brink.

Huge—and harmless to humans—the ocean sunfish or mola mola drifts near the surface of the open sea, feeding on jellyfish, plankton, and squid.

adapt—To change or develop in ways that aid survival in the environment.

algae—A one-celled or multicelled organism—generally found in water—that needs light to make energy through photosynthesis.

anatomy—Physical structure.

ancestral—Having to do with lines of descent or earlier forms.

aquatic—Inhabiting water.

conservation—Action or movement aimed at protecting and preserving wildlife or its habitat.

derived—Descended from earlier or ancestral forms.

ectothermic—Cold-blooded, dependent on heat sources outside the body.

evolution—The process by which new species, or types of plants and animals, develop from old ones over time.

evolve—To change over time.

extinct—No longer existing; died out.

fishes—Often used by scientists as the plural form for types, or species, of fish.

genetic—Having to do with genes, material made of DNA inside the cells of living organisms. Genes carry information about inherited characteristics from parents to offspring and determine the form of each organism.

ichthyology—The scientific study of fish.

marine—Inhabiting the ocean or a body of salt water.

microscopic—Extremely small; seen clearly (or at all) only through a microscope.

notochord—The flexible rod that protects the spinal nerves in some animals that lack backbones; early form of a backbone.

organism—Any living thing.

paleontology—The study of ancient life, mainly through fossils.

pesticide—Something that kills organisms considered to be pests by humans.

taxonomy—The scientific system for classifying living things, grouping them in categories according to similarities and differences, and naming them.

terrestrial—Inhabiting land.

vertebrate—An animal with a segmented backbone (the category also includes some organisms that have a notochord, or flexible rod of cells, instead of a spinal column made of bone).

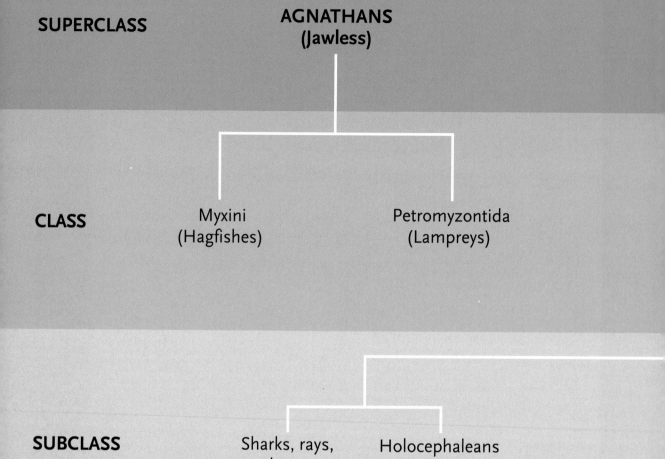

SUPERCLASS AGNATHANS (Jawless)

CLASS Myxini (Hagfishes) Petromyzontida (Lampreys)

SUBCLASS Sharks, rays, skates Holocephaleans (Chimaeras)

FAMILY TREE

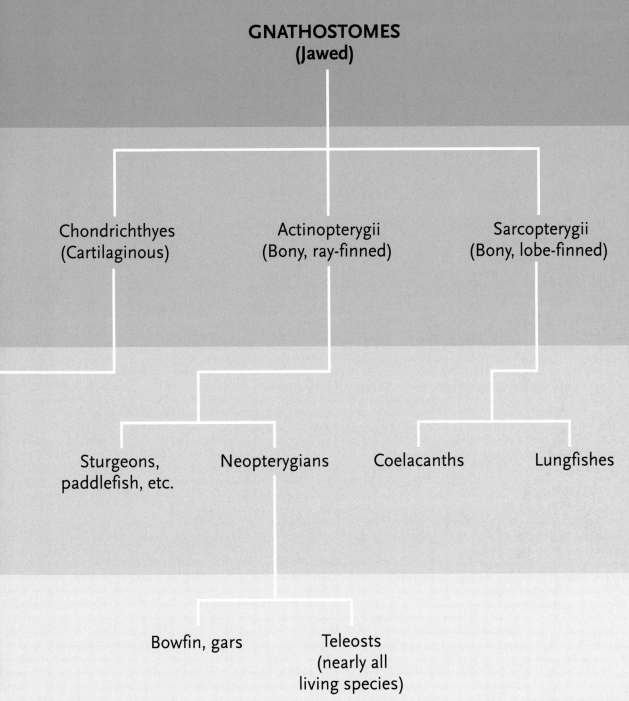

GNATHOSTOMES
(Jawed)

Chondrichthyes
(Cartilaginous)

Actinopterygii
(Bony, ray-finned)

Sarcopterygii
(Bony, lobe-finned)

Sturgeons,
paddlefish, etc.

Neopterygians

Coelacanths

Lungfishes

Bowfin, gars

Teleosts
(nearly all
living species)

F U R T H E R   R E A D I N G

Aquatic Life of the World. 11 volumes. New York: Marshall Cavendish, 2001.

Cerullo, Mary J. *The Truth About Dangerous Sea Creatures.* San Francisco: Chronicle, 2003.

Dipper, Frances. *Extraordinary Fish.* New York: DK Publishing, 2001.

Kurlansky, Mark. *The Cod's Tale.* New York: Putnam, 2001.

Morgan, Sally. *Fish.* Chicago: Raintree, 2005.

Parker, Steve. *Fish.* New York: Dorling Kindersley, 2000.

Sieswerda, Paul. *Sharks.* New York: Benchmark Books, 2002.

Walker, Sally M. *Fossil Fish Found Alive: Discovering the Coelacanth.* Minneapolis, MN: Carolrhoda, 2002.

W E B   S I T E S

http://www.livescience.com/fish
   This page is a portal to dozens of articles and photo galleries dealing with all aspects of fish behavior, biology, and conservation.

http://www.digitalfishlibrary.org/about_ichthyology/
   The Digital Fish Library is a partnership among several research institutions to create an online catalog of fish organized by order, family, and species, with an overview of ichthyology and fish evolution.

http://www.seaworld.org/Aquademics/tetra/all_about_fish.htm
Prepared by Seaworld, this "All About Fish" site offers a wealth of detailed information about bony fish, geared to students.

http://www.flmnh.ufl.edu/fish/Education/GroupsFish/FishGroups.htm
The Florida Museum of Natural History's Ichthyology pages give an overview of the classes of modern fishes, illustrated with photographs. The site is especially strong on information about sharks and fish native to Florida.

http://filaman.ifm-geomar.de/identification/classlist.cfm
Fish Identification helps you identify a fish's correct class based on its physical features.

http://animaldiversity.ummz.umich.edu/site/accounts/classification/Vertebrata.html
Animal Diversity Web, maintained by the University of Michigan's Museum of Zoology, has information about fish biology, distribution, and more. The main entries are under Class Chondrichthyes and Class Actinopertygii, reached from this Vertebrata page.

http://www.dinofish.com
Fish Out of Time is dedicated to the coelacanth, with information about recent discoveries, details of conservation efforts, and even a virtual coelacanth-cam.

http://evolution.berkeley.edu/evolibrary/news/060501_tiktaalik
Part of the University of California at Berkeley's Understanding Evolution site, this page on *Tiktaalik* highlights the exciting recent discovery of a fossil link between fishes and land animals.

The author found these books and articles especially helpful when researching this volume.

Barton, Michael. *Bond's Biology of Fishes.* 3rd edition. Belmont, CA: Thomson Brooks/Cole, 2007.

Clack, Jennifer. *Gaining Ground: The Origin and Evolution of Tetrapods.* Bloomington: Indiana University Press, 2002.

Long, John A. *The Rise of Fishes: 500 Million Years of Evolution.* Baltimore: Johns Hopkins University Press, 1995.

Mojetta, Angelo. *Sharks: The History and Biology of the Lords of the Sea.* San Diego, CA: Thunder Bay Press, 1997.

Moyle, Peter B. and Joseph J. Cech, Jr. *Fishes: An Introduction to Ichthyology.* 5th edition. Upper Saddle River, NJ: Prentice Hall, 2004.

Mydans, Seth. "Big-fish quest starts with real whopper." *Oregonian.* August 28, 2005.

Nash, J. Madeleine. "Our Cousin the Fishapod." *Time.* April 17, 2006.

Nelson, Joseph S. *Fishes of the World.* 4th edition. New York: Wiley, 2006.

Reebs, Stéphan. *Fish Behavior: In the Aquarium and In the Wild.* Ithaca, NY: Cornell University Press, 2001.

Wade, Nicholas, editor. *The New York Times Book of Fish.* Guilford, CT: Lyons Press, 2002.

Wilson, Steven G. "The Biggest Fish." *Natural History.* Vol. 115, Number 3, April 2006.

INDEX

Page numbers in **boldface** are illustrations.

A B O U T   T H E   A U T H O R

Rebecca Stefoff is the author of a number of books on scientific subjects for young readers. She has explored the world of plants and animals in Marshall Cavendish's Living Things series and in several volumes of the AnimalWays series, also published by Marshall Cavendish. For the Family Trees series, she has authored books on primates, flowering plants, amphibians, birds, marsupials, and fungi. Stefoff has also written about evolution in *Charles Darwin and the Evolution Revolution* (Oxford University Press, 1996), and she appeared in the *A&E Biography* program on Darwin and his work. Stefoff lives in Portland, Oregon. You can learn more about her and her books at www.rebeccastefoff.com.